HAL•LEONARD

pro vocal®
BETTER THAN KARAOKE!

SONGBOOK & SOUND-ALIKE CD
WITH UNIQUE *PITCH-CHANGER*™

Songs in the Style of
Nat "King" Cole

CONTENTS

Page	Title	DEMO TRACK	SING-ALONG TRACK
30	GEE BABY, AIN'T I GOOD TO YOU	1	9
2	I FOUND A MILLION DOLLAR BABY (IN A FIVE AND TEN CENT STORE)	2	10
6	IT'S ONLY A PAPER MOON	3	11
10	MAKIN' WHOOPEE!	4	12
14	ROUTE 66	5	13
18	THERE IS NO GREATER LOVE		
22	UNFORGETTABLE		
26	THE VERY THOUGHT OF YOU		16

Cover Photo: © Photofest Digital Library

ISBN 978-1-4234-6050-3

HAL•LEONARD®
CORPORATION
7777 W. BLUEMOUND RD. P.O. BOX 13819 MILWAUKEE, WI 53213

Visit Hal Leonard Online at
www.halleonard.com

I Found a Million Dollar Baby
(In a Five and Ten Cent Store)

from FUNNY LADY
**Written by Billy Rose, Mort Dixon
and Harry Warren**

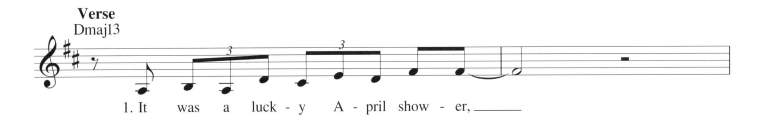

1. It was a luck-y A-pril show-er,

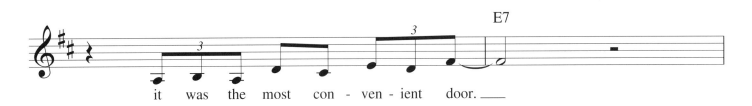

it was the most con-ven-ient door.

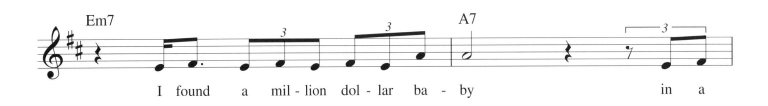

I found a mil-lion dol-lar ba-by in a

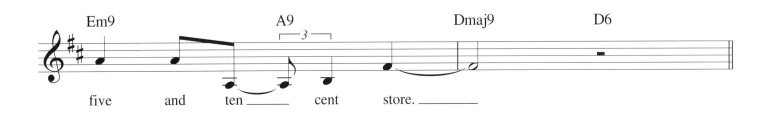

five and ten cent store.

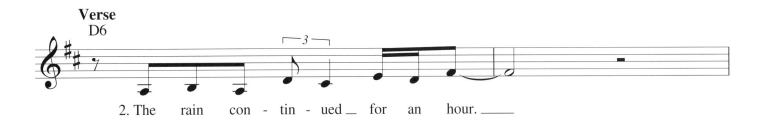

2. The rain con-tin-ued for an hour.

just step in - side _____ my cot - tage door ____

and ___ meet the mil - lion dol - lar ba - by ____ from the

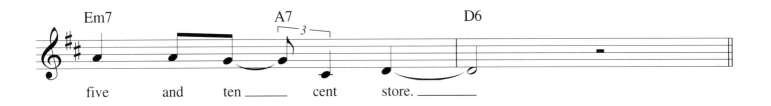

five and ten _____ cent store. _____

Interlude

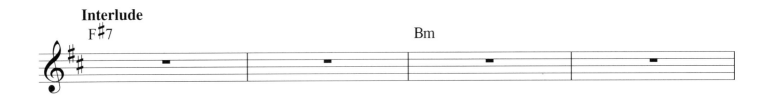

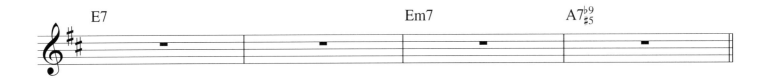

Verse

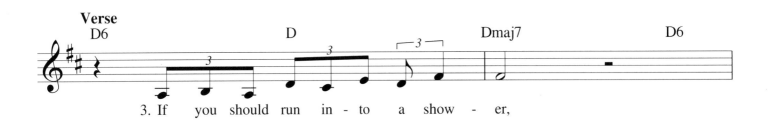

3. If you should run in - to a show - er,

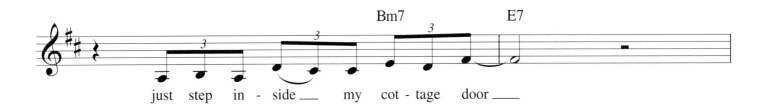

just step in - side __ my cot - tage door ____

and ___ meet the mil - lion dol - lar ba — by

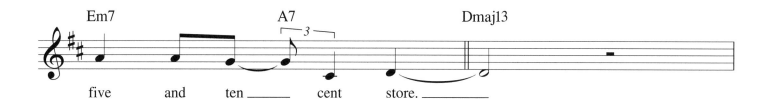

five and ten ____ cent store. _____

I ____ met a mil - lion dol - lar ba - by __

in the five

and

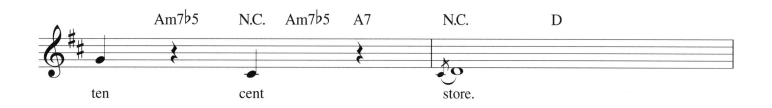

ten cent store.

It's Only a Paper Moon

featured in the Motion Picture TAKE A CHANCE
Lyric by Billy Rose and E.Y. "Yip" Harburg
Music by Harold Arlen

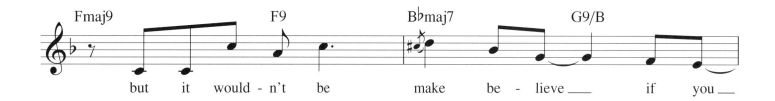

but it would-n't be make be-lieve ____ if you ____

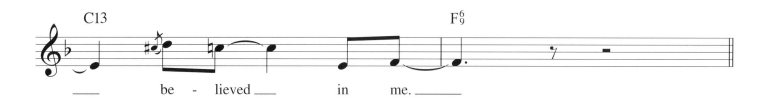

____ be-lieved ____ in me. _____

Interlude

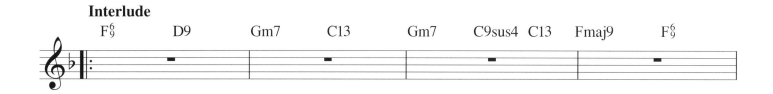

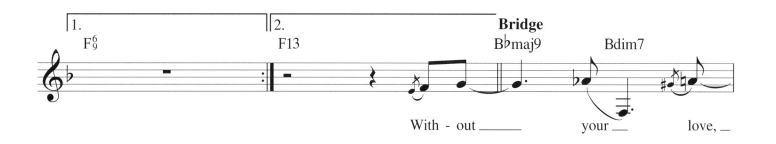

With - out _____ your ____ love, ____

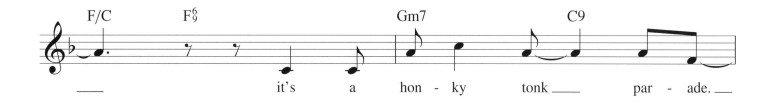

____ it's a hon - ky tonk ____ par - ade. ____

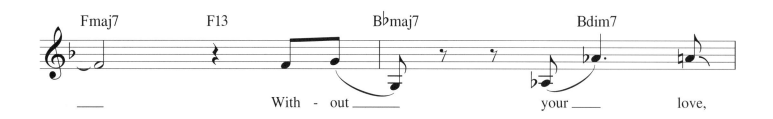

With - out _____ your ____ love,

Makin' Whoopee!

from WHOOPEE!

Lyrics by Gus Kahn
Music by Walter Donaldson

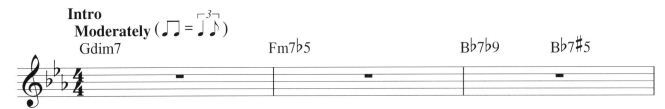

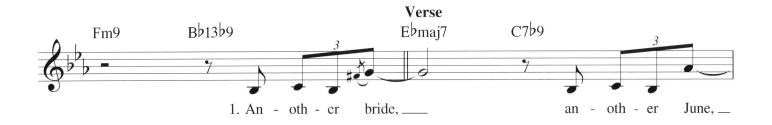

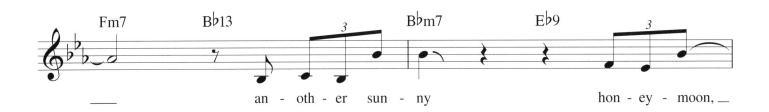

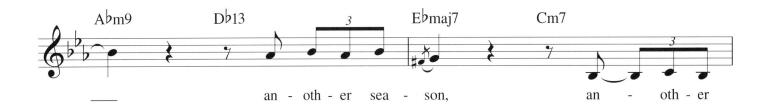

clothes, ___ he's so am - bi - tious, he ev - en sews, ___ ___ but don't for - get, folks, that's ___ what you get, folks, for mak - in' whoop - ee. ___

Interlude

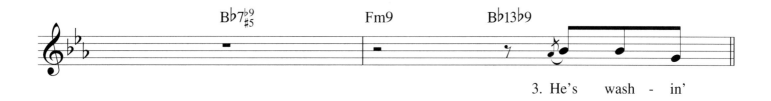

3. He's wash - in'

Verse

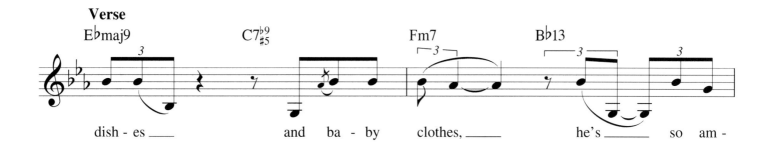

dish - es ____ and ba - by clothes, ____ he's ____ so am -

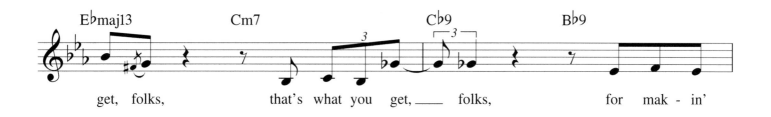

bi - tious, he e - ven sews, ___ but don't for -

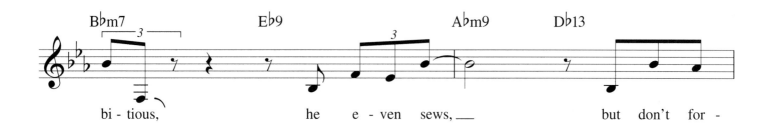

get, folks, that's what you get, ___ folks, for mak - in'

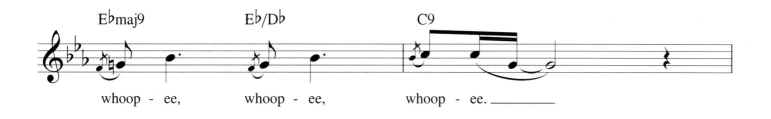

whoop - ee, whoop - ee, whoop - ee. _____

Route 66

by Bobby Troup

Interlude

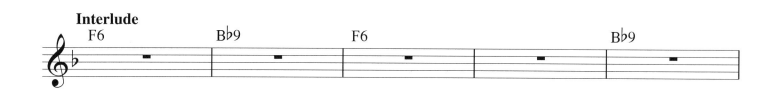

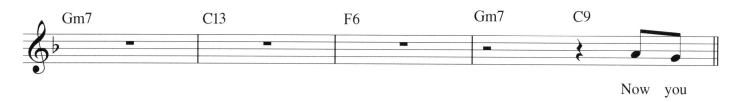

Now you

Bridge

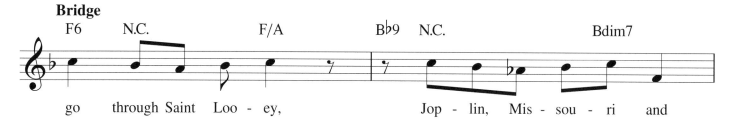

go   through Saint Loo - ey,   Jop - lin, Mis - sou - ri and

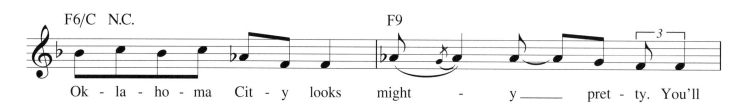

Ok - la - ho - ma Cit - y looks   might - y ____ pret - ty. You'll

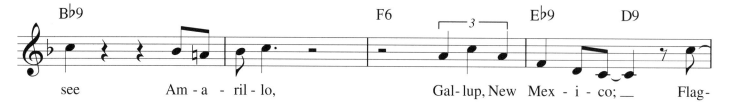

see   Am - a - ril - lo,   Gal - lup, New Mex - i - co; __   Flag-

16

-staff, Ar - i - zo - na, don't __ for - get Wi - no - na, King -

Verse

- man, Bar - stow, San Ber - nar - di - no. Won't __ you get hip __

__ to this time - ly tip, __ when you make that

Cal - i - for - nia trip? __ Get your kicks _

__ on Route ___ Six - ty Six. __ Get your kicks _

Outro

___ on Route ___ Six - ty Six. __ Get your kicks _

_____ on Route ___ Six - ty Six. __

There Is No Greater Love

Words by Marty Symes
Music by Isham Jones

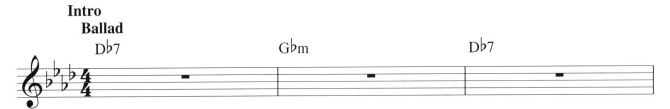

Verse

A♭

2. There is no great - er thrill _____

D♭7   C7

than   what   you   bring _____   to   me,

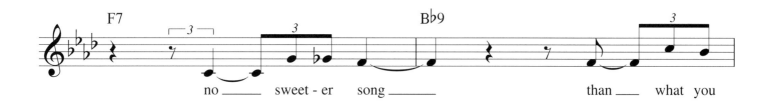

F7   B♭9

no _____ sweet - er   song _____   than ___ what you

G♭7   A♭6

sing   to   me. _____

Bridge

C7

You're ___ the   sweet - est   thing _____

D♭/F   Fm   C7

___   I   have   ev - er ____   known, ___

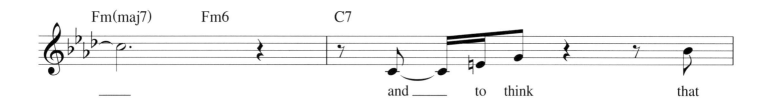

Fm(maj7)   Fm6   C7

___   and _____ to think   that

you are mine, ___ a - lone.

Verse

3. There ___ is ___ no great - er love

in all the world, it's true,

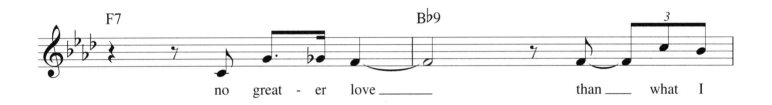

no great - er love ___ than ___ what I

feel for you. ___

Interlude

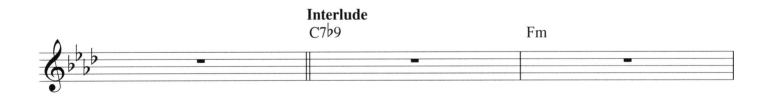

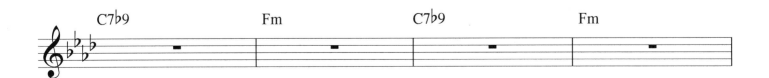

Bb13   Eb7

3. There   is   no

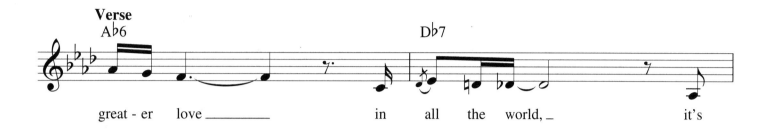

Verse
Ab6   Db7

great - er love _____ in all the world, _ it's

C7   F7

true,   no great - er love _____

Bb9   *rit.* Gb7

_____ than what I feel for

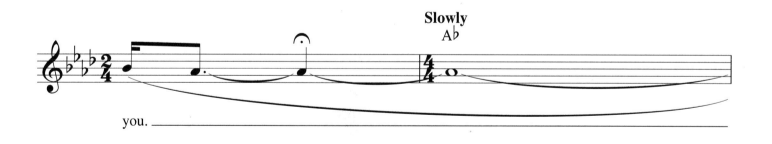

Slowly
Ab

you. _____

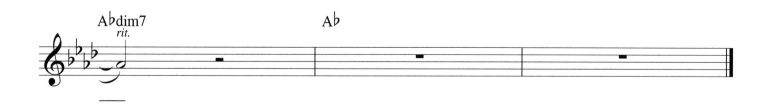

Abdim7   Ab
rit.

____

Unforgettable

Words and Music by Irving Gordon

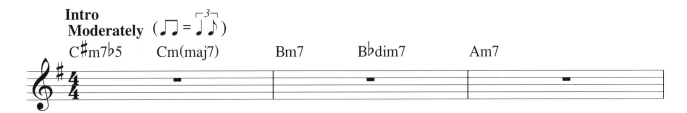

1. Un - for - get - ta - ble, _____ that's what _____

_____ you are. _____ Un - for - get - ta - ble, _____

_____ though near or _____ far.

Like a song of love _____ that clings _____ to me,

how the thought of you _____ does things _____ to me.

Nev - er ___ be - fore ___ has ___ some - one ___ been ___

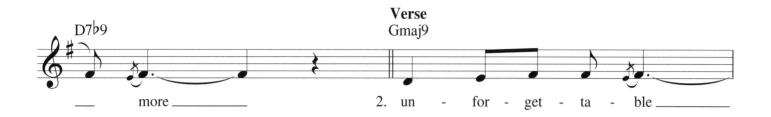

___ more ___ 2. un - for - get - ta - ble ___

Verse

___ in ___ ev - 'ry ___ way, ___

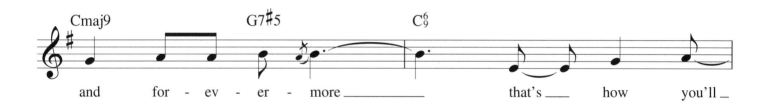

and for - ev - er - more ___ that's ___ how you'll ___

___ stay. ___ That's why, ___ dar - ling,

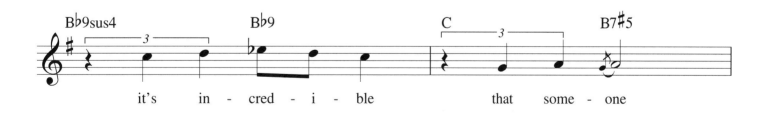

it's in - cred - i - ble that some - one

so un - for - get - ta - ble ___ thinks that I am

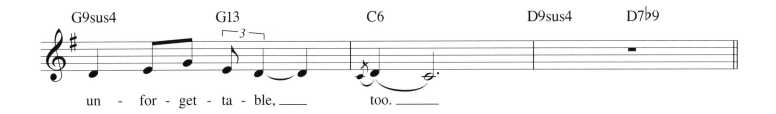

un - for - get - ta - ble, ___ too. ___

Interlude

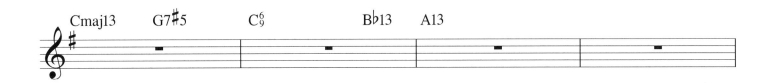

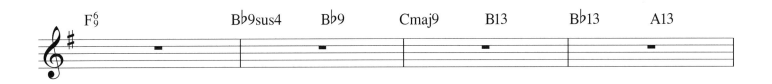

Verse

2. Un - for - get - ta - ble ___ in ev - 'ry ___

___ way, ___ and for - ev - er - more ___

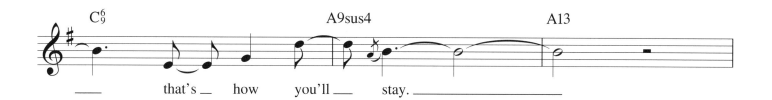

that's __ how you'll __ stay. _____

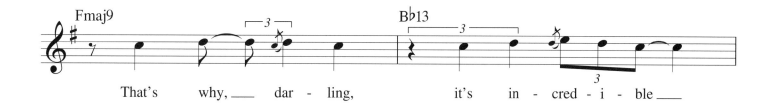

That's why, __ dar - ling, it's in - cred - i - ble __

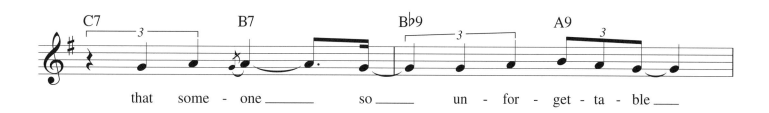

that some - one _____ so ____ un - for - get - ta - ble ___

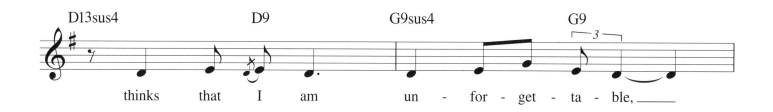

thinks that I am un - for - get - ta - ble, _____

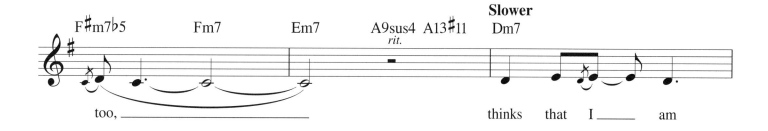

too, _____ thinks that I _____ am

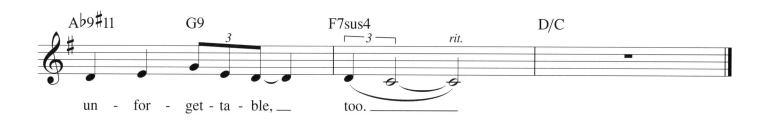

un - for - get - ta - ble, __ too. _____

The Very Thought of You

Words and Music by Ray Noble

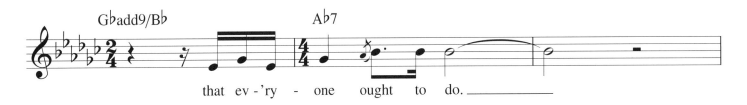

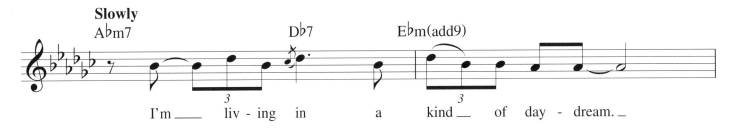

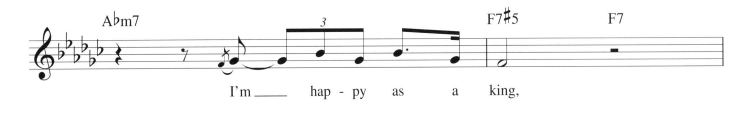

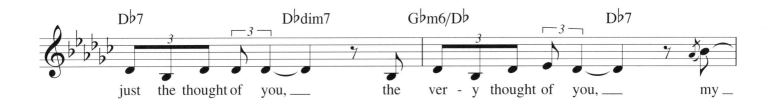

just the thought of you, ___ the ver-y thought of you, ___ my ___

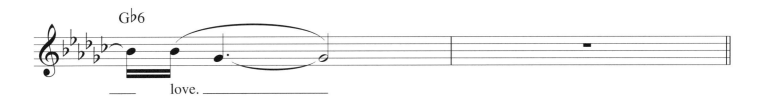

___ love. ___

Interlude

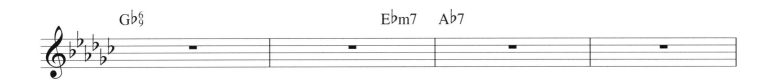

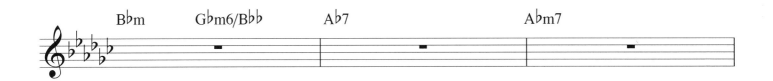

Verse

2. The mere i - de - a of you, ___

the long - ing here for you.

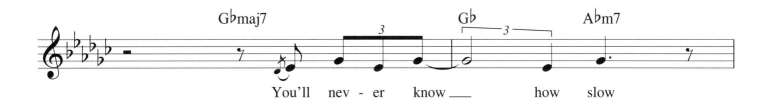

You'll nev - er know ___ how slow

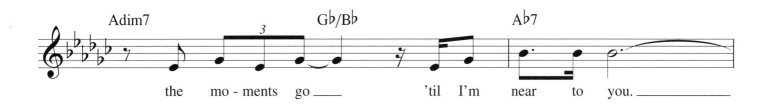

the mo - ments go ___ 'til I'm near to you. ___

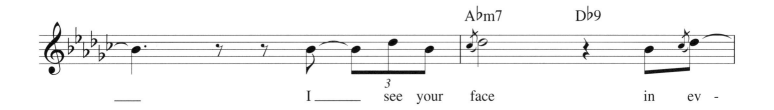

___ I ___ see your face in ev -

- 'ry flow - er, ___ your eyes ___ in stars a -

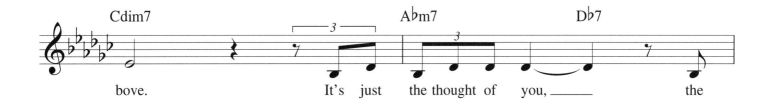

bove. It's just the thought of you, ___ the

ver - y thought of you, ___ my ___ love. ___

Gee Baby, Ain't I Good To You

Words by Don Redman and Andy Razaf
Music by Don Redman

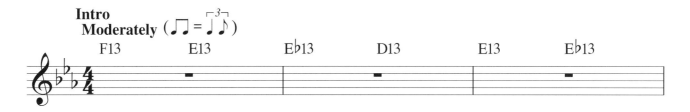

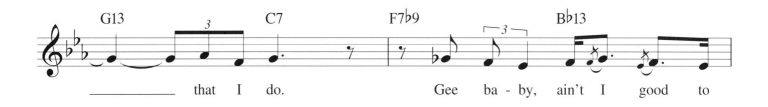

'Bought you a fur coat for Christ-mas, and a dia - mond ring, ___

big Cad - il - lac car, and ev - 'ry - thing. ___

Verse

3. What makes me treat you ___ the way ___ that I do? ___ Gee... ___

Slower

...ba - by, ain't I good to you?